WILDE CENTENARY POEMS

I Only Know That
I Love
Strength
In My Friends
And
Greatness

D1745156

James Liddy

Afterword by Michael S. Begnal

ARLEN
HOUSE

Collection © James Liddy 2003
Afterword © Michael S. Begnal 2003

The moral rights of the author have been asserted

First published by Arlen House in July 2003

Arlen House
PO Box 222
Galway
Ireland

42 Grange Abbey Road
Baldoyle
Dublin 13

ISBN 1–903631–44–0 paperback

arlenhouse@ireland.com
www.arlenhouse.com

Typesetting: Arlen House
Printed by: ColourBooks, Baldoyle, Dublin 13

contents

Dedication

for Bunny & Eric

acknowledgments

Some of these poems have appeared in *The Blue Canary, Orbis, Natural Bridge, Stinging Fly.*

I Only Know That
I Love
Strength
In My Friends
And
Greatness

"A Coat"

for Joan Navarre

Denny Fisher's story. Lady Hanson's
drawing room he came from the rain,
sat on the couch. Something lying
there. Lady Hanson said, "Don't sit
on Oscar's coat".

John Montague's. After
a reading in Philadelphia
an old man came with a coat
in his hands, "An Irish poet?
My great uncle was from
Dublin, Peter Doyle, Walt
Whitman's friend. This is
Walt's coat".

A coat carries its songs inside it
The emperor wears clothes years afterwards
the emperor wants to hand a coat to a friend

the only emperor is the emperor of need
that walks with you on a grey day
garment shiny as snow.

The emperor thinks about a great coat
can you hide a nightingale in its pocket
the male's melodious night song?

Many a king's son many a coathanger
has come at last to bare nakedness,
many a coat hanging many a body

(unheated 19th century weather
gods goddesses swop clothes among
    themselves,
the American swimteam ended that)

so Great Asterisk,
when you come back what kind of
outer garment will be in your wardrobe,
    monsignor?

Baudelaire liked to wear worn clothing –
patches along snowy quais –
the only coat is the coat which leads the
    dance.

An Anodyne

Descending to goldsand, cars, cops.

Descending the steps to the lake
from the Bistro, lines in moonlight
on water: moonlight better than
candlelight. Under a leaf
near the balustrade
the eyes maybe of Arthur Rimbaud.

You said at the table you hate summer,
"I want my body to stay white".
Your white body in a cool cave
that is a postcard on a grand piano,

what words do we leave out when
we play or chant through Lake Michigan?

Touch the coat over your heart
place my swimming mind on my hand on
    your heart,

Identities descend
past Ides through Kalends via these waves
    below
on Cream City beach,

no swans nor Romans,

though we are sometimes aghast
let us be lunar
on the grand staircase of the Wisconsin
    Republic
so at the bottom
we may be wood peasants in off light.

Water on a piano's keys.
Postcard near a lake.

Dans La Voiture Rouge Dans Le Stationnement

In car dark I propose
the veneration of images
the divination of images on paper
also adherence to non-images

besides I'm inefficient and awkward
in saying anything
a little shy even after drink
and you're worse than me

My compliment to you
you're as good a drunken driver as I used be

God make a star
out of each of us
on the front seats
in the sky on the page
just in a sentence
say stars in just
a footnote say that's us

Late
Night
Trilogy

LATE NIGHT NOTES

I went into the house, after waiting at the door
for your car warm-up thinking of running
over to it, and now it's 5 a.m. I think: my
mother said when I was born I cried for six
months, be merciful to one worn over a week
of christfeeding drinking, I was tired too from
the womb when I was born and they could
only stop me crying by driving around in the
car until I fell asleep, and next week I will fall
asleep in the beautiful red car and wake in
heaven.

The Yeats trick at Christmas is to "find the
bestial space" on the floor, and then to be that
raw bawling object until the car starts.

The angel Gabriel went to and from womb, I
whisper on the Dolls' road.

We'll have your mother's yule log yet when
Leif Erickson's boat Jimmy Boswell's carriages
pull in.

I think W. will not destroy us.

No Blood Axe at Christmas but Leif Erickson
in vestments at mass in Juneau Park. In
any case heroes and wine.

FURTHER LATE NIGHT NOTES

I want to take your mother to Mayfields for
Christmas. Be a Scots about the tree its
caressing arms, but remember for the ten
years of Cromwell's rule no Nativity, the
theatres closed, the drinking age was 55.

Good will rabbitjump out of the gold bare
hands of the tree. Love catches it.

I remember late night hours in the little red
car with the embossed Byzantium seats, I am
imagining as usual true religion.

"Since my childhood I have not wanted
anything else but to receive the complete
revelation of this before dying". Simone Weil
sends a gold star over the doll's house, the car
runs down the giant's causeway.

LATE NIGHT SABBATH NOTE

Teacher against sobriety.

Fr. Mike quotes bartender voice in the Gospel.
A good bartender saves the world.

"Houses will be divided over me, parents
    against children ..."
The last best wine.

"It not going to be peaceful, it's not going to
heaven. 12 years ago I got the symptoms of
AIDS, sore throat, spots, night sweats,
between Thanksgiving and Christmas
I lost 37 pounds. I've got to tell Mom. I said to
myself I hope it's cancer because if it is
everyone will say, 'Poor father Mike, he did a
good job, he was funny, he helped a lot of
people', but if it's AIDS they'll say, 'Father
was fooling around'. I was ashamed of the
thought".
 "Sibling against sibling".

Understanding a person or idea with
    desire/after desire

with a glass in your hand or an imaginary
   glass.
"Arm yourself".

Jesus bartender voice says, stop thinking
   about families.

[UNTITLED]

Four attitudes towards the idol.
Adoration, attack, abasement, atonement (that
    takes longer),
then I would kneel by the armchair,
on her carpet.
First two of the above the Pagan Yeats dance
the last two the Catholic Pieta dance I do in
    the malls of my
recriminating life, a writhing motion. Written
    flower drooped
on the floor!

The Magi voted for Al,
that's more important
than how the dolls voted.

I know how you voted
but I don't know how
the dolls voted.

(I wonder who is the
Patron Saint of paranoia …
Pius XII couldn't make up
his mind on this …)

Election day for reports.
Those dolls have never done
enough screaming or
dancing on students' papers,

if the dolls ran away
we would follow them
to the only floor feet
know, Barwood Arcady.

I place pints beside you
raise glasses
heart on splurging elbows:

"Some living dolls know I vote
against the neighbours,
those windy bagpipe folk".

TO THE METAL

I'm using the word "gold", most of the
stations of the day, I pan your mind cells,
your internal system, grains of ordinary
existence turn into gold – not your body
exactly which may be but gold dust. A hoard
of depth, of gazes – it is the unique average
situation. I use a word to embellish the
everything of anything.

Maybe it needs a certain kind of cunning to
have gold-eyes for the speck in your
neighbour's eye. A clue, the one who is nearly
all gold does not know.

To rephrase in such a way that belief is linked.
We do not understand it at first as
glorification occurs. Glorification means to
adore, you don't like this, nobody rational
can, not even the shepherds of pastoral

– this is far from Constitutional entombment. The smile of Ramses at Thebes is not the same as Voltaire's. The aroma of the bazaar is missing from "enlightenment", and unsparing twilight. From morning's arc to evening's swing, the body just touches the spirit's embrace. Just turns it –

this is not Deist/anti-Deist talk, I wear the collar of gold in your valley of colour.

CLARIFICATIONS ABOUT A
HOUSE SOLD IN 2002

Gold womb house
I never sickened or died in
but it touches cold as her death
faded Chippendale and Queen Anne wall
    bracket,
a garden sometimes kept though the tennis
    court went
where flower space and scent space are given
    majestic rent
today two roses and buttercups of the new
    century –
a lot came out of this, time spent climbing up
    damp walls
poems' origins cavorting in Georgian voodoo,
we will lie together in the grave this house
    and I –
It was far from
"swanning" the country phrase meaning a
    young man
preparing for woman on the mating spell
    river
lost in plumage …
Set down thy matriarchy:
New York money, immigrant princess
    rascality,
half-interested intermittent Venus shell in
    darkness

bedroom hangover gathered to thick
trembling unity utterly uncertain of effect.
Her holding luminous memory unknowing if
    the mirror looks back
Irish-American first generation marvels
locked in a country doctor's house,
your objection to dying: you wouldn't know
    how the furniture would do
at the auction. Clare, the sideboard in the hall
    fetched ten thousand pounds.
Josie, get the champagne glasses.
We set up a duet at a crushed sorrow's pace
eyes look long at each other we lose our
    bodily appearances
I hold your memory for the only moment that
    is in this world
first clarifications and then charities;
we are designated to put signatures to a
    manifesto of delicacy
made up poured from a pitcher of culture
    echoes,
out on the street up from post-earthly
bar question and answer cycle
beneath arriving cunning summer foliage.
Swallows dive in the yard yet the god of the
    vanished summer house
out in the garden still mutters at me
over the ghost croquet mallets
in Latin but I translate,
"Blockhead this is where you found love and
    death join".

Hans Christian

Do we know a fairy tale
is as beautiful as a Christmas tree?
The fairy tale sparing and unsparing
of human beings.
Consider how circular our bridges
are, this is "the road of a thousand wonders".
I should wear my Citta del Vaticano
cap for luck?
I will never, never, forget how circular
the love bridge is, fairy tales demonstrate
straight bridges don't exist.
This is enough of camera on someone!
This was a postcard.

[UNTITLED]

Almost as if your poems were Collected
    Bulbs.
I felt the words on these bulbs pumping,
on the cold street they shivered. I feel like
slipping into these singing bulbs, careful not
to break any of them. Another night of
    ornaments.

I bring a flower
to Enderis
blue.

On being asked what colour pyjamas
he would like in heaven
or what kind of bikini he would wear
on the Kaiser's birthday

cobalt blue.

My first flowers.

A question; do you think mermaids and
    mermen
hang out at Patti's?

The history of our lives:
Christmas tree
the angel Gabriel
the couch Garbo sat on in Patti's,
glasses of many colours,
A lake where it is impossible to tell
whether it is an angel on the way to The
    Virgin Mary
or a mermaid on the way to a merman or a
    mermaid.

Look: two animal souls
without cave images
a flower in hand
blue.

A man maketh a tower
he hath his rooms painted cobalt blue
Thor Ballylee's walls …

Someone walks out of Enderis Hall
my blue-veined man!

NOT BEING AT TYLER'S READING

I thought Morris dancing the nearest to
feeling poetry in your ankles 1957

In the Brown Jacket bookshop as I was a
laurel-wreather hearing people
talking about me not going to poetry readings
1963

Old dreamers like Proust sit through the night
on couches that are never soiled

Entangle themselves in carriages and woods

Proust all night in a carriage near the forest's
entrance gate

Elegance of dreaming alone about one

He came to read at half way dream house in
white body light

Pearls on leaves after the walk from the door
to the gate

He is my mot lifting a white finger on a leaf.

But worship from afar was always songs
anyway

Time past wreaths mutter a reading once a
year when he will sing Morrissey
who is a Morris dancer's ghost 1999

CASEY'S BIRTHDAY LIST FOR SEAMUS
(JULY)

A talk about love on the tennis court steps
Other translations of Baudelaire
Ice cream
Desserts for dinner
A morning in Morocco
Two postcards of Oscar Wilde
scribbling on the back

Seamus's birthday list for Casey (August)
Pens and inks
A signed photograph of Morrissey
A flask
Crunchy bars
A nude portrait by Paul Funge
Goth clothes
Twilight in Glasgow

CHER C,

Literature first, it is a Masque of Themes.
Some floating off the Normandy beach, some
a-drift in bistros, something in the rotting
orchards along the Ebro.

This was meant to be a passionate letter
from Lorca but as often happened with him
it became a letter of despair.

Why, after such nights in such gardens/
cities you won't communicate with me
I don't know, I know you very well
but why you don't do things I'm not sure.

To see you are composed of light,
that is what love is, but there is
another element in the world, that is
not doing some things you don't do
loses out Light stays with itself.

It is as if I had died reading
the obituary of Brian Moore
at the Madrid departure gate, if I had
not woken on the plane, if I had not

made it in the retired cop car up 94,
if we had died eating chorizo in Lou Bruno's.

But if I was a ghost wouldn't you want to
meet me? Because if you didn't want to meet
with my ghost that would be your failure.

[UNTITLED]

Springtime, you know where

Take a poem to Les Invalides

be sure Napoleon reads it
be sure the King of Rome hears

Recommended a long tipple
in the cafés run
by the same families
for a hundred years

be sure there are paradises
they are returnable

you're a paradise boy
your white shirt makes Parisians
think you're a tennis player

Breton was a wuss you know
he never wrote for the nipple
(take that poem)

An American doesn't stop walking
on the quais of the Elysian Fields
O beautiful shoulder
chest

Dance there

Small women in black
men in almost black
with dyed black hair
every one into music
so cool there's no discussion
the response must be dangerous wisdom
a kind of French wisdom
cranky comradeship
that blows night backwards and forwards

that delays morning's dew-work
no aggressive grace holds everyone back
reading writing gives the black eye of
      astonishment
you find a beautiful sound in the sentence
when you hear that you write
when a page announces what a friend should
      say
a book has the eyes of a lover
Do the black eye dance for ever

To the Chevalier

O the songs of the love waiters and waitresses
through the Parknasilla furze bushes

O the railway carriage my mother sat in on
    the way
to Parknasilla while the last Chief Secretary of
    Ireland
poured blandishments in her earring

O the nights of the Kerry anarchist narcissists
    cavorting on the goat-swarmed stage

O the sparks the echoes the expectant footfalls
    from the random raths of mirth

O the perfect onanistic moment prone in the
    boat outside Tarbert harbour

O the berth of an afternoon Shelbourne
    lounge-hand grazing a knee

O men like skittles along the Seine

O roselips taken from Yeats's easel

O Dedalus jigged in the wine jug

(Samsweetman)

O Telemachus O Paris I hardly knew you in
the Quarter sheets of dawn

In summer faraway in the balding New World
in a hundred degrees in the garden of vodka
    lemonades
outside the bar I serenade you boulevard-set
    Chevalier

Health to both our afterwards

Territorial
Poems

THE TERRITORY OF ENID STARKIE
AND RIMBAUD

C'est moi began writing so beautifully in the
1870's that poetry became C'est moi even if it
wasn't as beautiful. But it did better than
before. It became a list of lovers, if not quite
that it stuttered as a list of drinks. There are
two sailor suits in this story and they were
never worn on the same day or in the same
navy. One was worn on the Seine and on the
Thames.

Miss Enid wore hers walking down the main
street in Roundstone, Galway. Jesus, Mary,
and Enid. The little roads of the heart bracing
itself for the gypsy frying pan.

This would be the winter of Moi's fretting
about his vials in Africa.

Miss Enid walked in Connaught free of
horrors, a woman in a sailor suit, hurt as a
woman a long time in a pigmy Anglo-Irish
West.

Moi stepping in company of nomads to their
wells.

In Sommerville Miss Enid stayed in bed as she
hasn't a change of underwear, a lady's child.

I see them both taking a glass of champagne
the colour of the first plaster statue they
prayed to. They never interviewed each other
except in imaginary transepts.

The beautiful product and the saleswoman of
beauty. The sales talk. Publishers flogged the
books.

But Moi and Miss Enid wear sailor suits for
beauty not work. Tightrope for beauty not
exercise.

Moi whispers at last, "Under an African sun
Apollo reminisces".

THE TERRITORY OF JARRY

I want to hold on to your head as it's
summer's end kisses work the torso of faith to
a bleeding heart merged in the biggest stone
of The Circle where you lay your throbbing
head involved in the benediction of the pool
and sighs lift arms of need chests of need to
the one who may hear

St. Anne I will pilgrim and be your man so
find me a man sons of rich Breton farmers
strut by the pool wounded already by the
deathbent blessings stitched into starchy
smocks their little prayer books bent with
weapons of love by their swimming sides

Study to climb the stairs beyond the tiny saint
lake and find a man so much more beautiful
than me that will be carved of milk glasses
fresh from the cow I was made by woman's
genius and heavenly wells the law shines out
of shoes on water that is proved by Monsieur
Baudelaire's promenade in Jeanne's shoes
along the vestibules to the Seine

In lecture notes I read Baudelaire's life exactly
links with Kerouac's (compare) and both
perhaps rewrite the life St. Anne

For you summer man by the apartment's door
eternal trifle passes into the skin of my finger
a little blushing heart under the warts with a
little silver minnow I wed thee I wed thy
womanising body thy eyebrows like mini
crown of thorns thy dark foxred hair radiating
Jesus loopy curls lets dangle our troths by St.
Anne by the skeletons of the 30 martyrs under
the trapdoor the little weeds and small
flowers by water edges twist their heads and I
understand the aristos are martyrs for sexlove
I place the scroll of intrigue on the rolledout
street carpet

You wheel your bicycle to a stop put it under
the lamplight Jerod

Street shrine standing sun and moon of every
Eros day above the trapdoor owls kisses are
butterflies inside a cowl the great fairy parade
is on us in summer the Roman pagan saints
marching sun tongue and moon penises hoot
in shadows of Trepart exercise wear lingerie
door St. Anne send me a man of truly great
ambiguities I translate and sign the petition

Make summer resort of these lips repeat
summer repeat cowl butterflies

Hearts baking in stones

Plant two hot kisses on your lips your bicycle
waits

THE TERRITORY OF
WILLIAM BURROUGHS

Opposite sides of the wine and coffee strewn tables:

"Is flirtation flattery, is the lover reduced to the role of an entertaining tease?"

"Sometimes 'agents' tell me to relax, be yourself, express real feelings". "Damn agents. I feel like Lee when I approach others". "I have stretched truth to get things I want which doesn't exclude sex necessarily but do I feel right about it?"

"Caricatures – places depicted – in the dream are just that, a dream?" "Better not believe that, think T.B. Sanatoriums". "Some of us have been institutionalised for his and our safety?"
"Civil priorities!"

"Raying blue boy innocence with lizard blue or whatever colour. Pretending he is not wearing a mask among these airheads". "I

wish he would happen on a young man with
less narrow eyes".

"The lizard is both dangerous and venomous
and sweet and gentle, and if the boy would
give him a chance he would be the best friend
he could find, cliffs cafés or anywhere".

"I remember reading something of Kafka
about a penal colony. I picture the colony in
Norway or Sweden – maybe not though –
I don't think there are many lizards in areas
like that".

"I want a black lizard with beautiful violet
eyes ..."

THE TERRITORY OF KEROUAC

Je suis Cinderella
Je suis Votre Cinderella aussi
Heard you Beatrice
Salvation is how you sing
and dance on a visit
to The Virgin Mary
You can't go back to first prayers
you can make the sign of the cross
If you wish smear me with dung
yes smear me with dung
Jean d'Arc knelt on the coldest
stone in the chapel
Homeward all my angels
Blessed be brother and sister
trapped in my body
I dance on the good day
Je suis Notre Dame de Lourdes
Love is a Canon Law Code
Blessed be boyfriends
and girlfriends trapped in
brothers and sisters
Thomas Wolfe and Kirk
in a seedy elegant bistro
angel streams in window
I want to be the toughest
lovenik in town
Cold stone of the chapel
shipped to America

Charles de Gaulle's eyes
present arms to me
Je suis Quebec
with beads from Seine water
Yes pray for the bedbugs
Pope Paul is the grape of the vine
You can go home again to the bistro
I have no dance steps
the ballroom of the saints astonishes me
and the fires of Rouen
and the fires of Drancy
au dela du possible
au dela du connu
kneeling
invisible dance step
Je suis Bernadette Soubirous

The Territory of Jack Spicer

God be like God.
Marvels from lips:

Robin Blaser and Jack Spicer walking hear
Duncan reading in the distance during a
Berkeley Free Speech fête Blaser says, "Now
there is the great Duncan".

Jack Spicer was terrible in bed, Duncan
wanted to make love to everyone. "He slept
with me but then he slept with everyone".

After they got the house, Jess wouldn't let
Robert bring anyone home. That's why he was
a terror on the road.

Robert had a breakdown in Louisiana, had to
learn the alphabet over again. George visited
him, "Robert, I know you like Jane Austen but
I prefer George Eliot". Robert: "That's,
George, because you're a disciplinarian
whereas I'm a society lady".

George also visited Joanne Kyger. Joanne,
"Would you like a little smoke?" "Well, Jack
wouldn't approve but I guess he's dead".
They walked out to the back garden, there
were 8 feet high bamboo shoots. At least they
looked like bamboo: marijuana and they
smoked it.

Spicer simply was a great flirt.

Spicer never went to parties, but next day he
wanted to know what exactly happened.

Spicer hated beards. When Ebbe Boregaard
grew one Jack said, "That's a fake beard isn't
it, Ebbe?" Jack wasn't interested in anyone
with a beard.

In Gino and Carlo's like The Place he was in
love and drinking, sweetest sourest
intern/monk. Voice a casual stretching-back
voice lavished but lavished out of Chaucer's
Troilus, Marlowe's and Wescott's Leanders.

I that loved thee since my American life
began, most caressing enforcer of paragraphs
ever moulded by the lips of wobblies and
    cowboys.
Charlemagne was camp in San Francisco.

THE TERRITORY OF THE PLANTER
AND THE GAEL

This caper concerns "blossoming and
    dancing", we want to see
the dancers in the dance. Partner Elizabeth
    Bowen
and Medbh McGuckian on the floor. Asking
    them,
invite McGuckian in the daylight, approach
Bowen at night, she's tabooed, she's in the
    speakeasy.
"As long as I can remember I've been
    extremely conscious
of being Irish … I must say it's a highly
    disturbing emotion".
It takes an Irish person to know how difficult
    it is to be Irish.
She held up a varnished nail at the UCD
    English Literature Society,
"For years I used to go down the stairs to a
    London basement
and scratch on the window, Virginia Woolf
    admitted me to conversation".
By night in Dublin she put on red lipstick,
    wore a red dress.
Bowen like Jane in *The World of Love* was
    "tense with
suspended dew; her own beautiful
    restlessness was everywhere".

The aroma of desire, catalogued by Patricia
    Coughlan, fades in and out
out of her text. The meaning of *The World of
    Love* is – well – love.
The whimsical extraordinary set of moments
in *The Planter and the Gael*. Innumerable
word-strewn cries,
first half of a Bowen novel is hard then
    wonderful pages turn into
dewy driveways through grounds, with
    rereads
constant inspection of syntax image
    McGuckian begins to clear.
One tries to recuperate from the Anglos
the other defies the Anglo-Ulster set. I dream
    in North Cork
of a book written by a she, I dream in the
    North of a poem without an l.
I am alien and Dionysian and in my books my
    house is jammed
with lovers, I am alien primitive and
    Dionysian and my poems
curate portrait galleries where nude lovers
    flourish.
My men are drawing-room sparks, my men
    march in the doom-mist
of sublime revolt. I feel a sort of influence in
    the air
like the flame of a candle burning on saints'
    days,
my signature is as vibrational as parish
    flowers.
McGuckian deciphers until the morning, this
    is the reborn country,

these are her dance steps: gone former syntax
     present the ruin
of the narrative present sighs and ghost
     spakes.
McGuckian dedicates *Selected Poems* to Roger
     Casement
and the rebel Bowen declares when Mr.
     Churchill goes I go. Floor eyes
around the clock. White poppies (war) white
     feathers (cowardice) diamond bullets
(aristocracy rebellion) milordless (gentry
     gentillity wealth sex)
secret hand (dried sweet hard tears), marry
     dancers as they are.
Both writers people of the god and the goat
spikers of epics about solicitation as much as
     salvation. People
of the harp Janus-like facing both ways to the
     harp shaped graves
in briars and grass. Miss Welty on Bowen:
     Terra firma
implies the edge of the cliff. Miss Bowen Ms.
     McGuckian,
take each other's waist as dandies and
     dervishes.
Otherwise no galas de jour for Ireland.
Dance we must, dance we have to, even in
     circles like this.

THE TERRITORY OF
MICHAEL HARTNETT

Like Kavanagh out of the Irish earth
unstoppable. Whatever spotlighted these lads
riding wild horses, bards of a rural
Hollywood, beautifully violent violently
beautiful Music first in fields then for throats
divine and dry in public house ...

That kitchen. Jordan and I through Bishop
street ("without a bishop") Maiden street
("without a maiden"), in 28 Assumpta Park,
brothers at football, Dennis the father already
gone out going out again. Jordan Dean of
Letters gave Michael a pound a week for a
year, college plans, Dinny O'Dwyer, Paddy
Kavanagh, first caper at Poetry Ireland's
launch in the Bailey, Ben Kiely in braces Liam
Miller leading the chorus in poet-laden lanes.

We are figures in a mist, I think of him on the
Feast of the Epiphany, I see him again in
Grogan's.

He was drinking out of the skull of bards
further afield than Kerry.

Temple Bar Hotel 4 a.m. Allen Ginsberg wrote
a three page letter on Michael's poems, he
made a hundred copies and distributed them
at the top of Grafton Street.

Quinsworth were distributing free grapefruit
with South African wine, Pat rang up to say
he and Richard were quarreling; Michael went
over to help, grapefruit on the chairs, the
couch, the TV, "I'll have a glass".

He said to Nuala Ní Dhomhnaill he blamed
Natasha. "Natasha who?" "Natasha
Smirnoff".

Summer, what a way for a bard to go out, on
the phone!

Calls to Coolgreany, a call while I was in
O'Neill's, a call to Milwaukee: while Angela
was away his daughter had brought him over
lunch, an orange a bottle of vodka. He sang a
stave on Inchicore, recited a poem for me: a
carrot on a vegetable stand gets up, walks
across the road, and is crushed by a van.

Bog fairy country accent, lilting, looking like a
changeling, famished, dry, unstoppable.

From the day in the kitchen to the day in the
hospital Raifteirí and Merriman two pourers.
Wine in re-remembrance, less bread much
wine, wine by the ditch.

I place him on the border between Limerick
city and county. Hartnett closes the door,
walks by hedge and ditch, unbuttons his shirt,
eats the mushrooms and dew in the morning.

What hides in us is the priest.
What hides in us the gunman whether
        post-Jacobite or not.
Bogcotton our Court dress.
Queen-lavisher.
God-eater.
God-dipper.

October 15, 1999

(left to right) Liam O'Connor, Micheal Hartnett
and James Liddy in the early 1960s

(photo taken by Liam Miller)

THE TREE AND THE PARTY

Everything is owed to the devil's party,
Paul Funge broke the
monotony of good guy days
in after pub lark.

Borrowed Kirk's hat and danced with it,
attracted repulsed by Kirk's hairy legs
(shorts).

I have a principle: you let the devil's party
enter to make fun. To be able to say I gave
a lot of my life to kitchen dances.

Devil's parties anywhere, you carry a portable
kitchen around: Canadian writers
born in the US are in Dublin,
fun in the horseshoe lounge, £35 rounds.

Stan Persky George Stanley of Jack Spicer's
party!
Stan: Spicer was dangerous. He met you,
fell in love with you, wrote your poems for
you, channeled your poems by falling in love,
made an agony of it, that was the point.

I say now, I'm too old for romance,
I just want sex.

Dialogue at this devil's party:
J.L. So you and Spicer didn't …
Stan: Jack and I fooled around. Jack said,
I always take my tricks to breakfast.
At breakfast he said, good love, bad
lover.
J.L: Referring to …
Stan: Himself.
J.L. I hear by contrast Robert Duncan was
a god in bed.
George: Which god?

This information is important, Eric, to the future
of American poetry which will be written in this
century given the right gossip.

I have a principle: important poetry is
        impossible
to publish (kitchens in San Francisco nicer
than New York).

The tree we say goodbye under at night,
        Romeo-Juliet-
Godot branches, is a gossip tree. Its talking
        shadow
bends itself to after pub language.
Love sits in the party on its branches and

maybe
knows what to say? Learn to climb the gossip
    tree.
Climb with the alphabet.

THE GOREY ART FESTIVAL 1982

The night before the opening of the Tenth Festival.

"To enter the nineteen eighties of your own heart", M said to E adding a reference to what he had just been told about E's basking with some girls after dry months, "you're in a frieze with more than two figures walking in it". "It's the lack of company that killed me", E said, "there's no one here to discuss dreams or ideas with me, I should have been a civil servant or a priest or something".

"Oh", said M, "that's part of it, essentially we are priests, I seem an apostolic administrator to Dr. Faustus. Lorcan our boy poet over there Christ's uncorrupted face on an Art Centre wall, and you the hard-working deacon. But everything hangs by shins and veins".

E was talking to one of the girls. M closed his eyes and thought about how literature might take a bow, might travel down the Courtown or Carnew roads to people.

E was free again and M had something new:
"For some reason the festival makes me think
of the Pre-Reformation charismatic Hans
Boehm who rose against the church to keep
the church – it was going to get nailed
anyway. Hans is like our 'revered founder', he
would sit in taverns and teach naked".

M remembered what the Virgin Mary had
told Hans, "The time is approaching when all
the priests will be slain and anyone who kills
thirty of their number will be entitled to a
reward". E asked, "Do you think these
prophecies are continuing, though not as
bloodthirsty?" M replied, "The festival has
this magic, we hear voices and get grants,
tonight is the room of brothers, actual
apocalypse".

Out of the blue M leaned into the unoccupied
ear of E to say, "Maybe we will be the priests
then".

THE CABALA

The good cardinals
return to Catullus and Livy because they are
    stopped
at every Christian exit by slippered
    bureaucrats;
a consolation to a cardinal in old age is the
    sensual
dominance of poetry, the godlike chatter of
    great history.

In the sunlit garden of Wilder's they read and
    read.
The muses are people they discover, not all of
    them dead.
They don't want Horace's word only, they
    want to see
someone, the old age of cardinals is a glass in
    another's hand.

Meanwhile in the palace, there is no time for
    poems, they were
writing Encyclicals in less than punchy Latin.
    Our Lady
of Fatima waves her robe in the gardens, she
    also comes

to breakfast in the Pontiff's room. They talk
  science.

The cardinals who are not obsessive about *The
  Eclogues*
become toadies eavesdroping at the morning
  meal.
The Girl in the room and The Pope worry
  about Russia;
Cardinal Spellman will have to take care of it.

Cardinal Schuster, who got too few votes to be
  Pope, who
tried to get Mussolini sanctuary, runs the anti-
  court in Milan
(Martini now). He puts on the Mask of Ovid
  and gazes
at the river. Cardinal Tisserant studies Coptic
  texts,
holds a sword underneath for the day he will
  descend
as Cardinal Deacon and tap Pacelli's skull.

Through universal science, honeycombs, and
  birettas
Pacelli still walks quicker than anyone in
  procession of lace.
He barks on a golden telephone, "kneeling,
  Monsignor?"
Finally the Caesars are ladies, intelligent, tall,
  cranky.

The good cardinals still dream of poems that
    move like magi
or dolls. They think of the sighs of Jesus's
    donkey.
They wish they composed a poem that would
    start,
"Holy Father, pray for old rabbis, Max Jacob,
the sisters of Kafka, the prince and princess
of Hesse … Holy Father, go to the
    slaughterhouses and pray".

The cardinals who feel they could sit on a
    donkey's back
place Catullus's page beside a fourth glass of
    wine.
They look up and catch a glimpse of St.
    Peter's:
Oh, Gehenna, Gehenna!

Miss Byrne in the Post Office
sent each year a birthday card
to Pius XII, Vatican City. She showed it
to me for spelling and punctuation.

SISTER!

The room is of the boudoir.
Packages lie along the walls
alongside Yeats's paintings.

Clusters on the mantlepiece.
Sherry, kept at the back
of the room, is plentiful –

in the palace in Madrid with
Miss Moran, governess to the royal
children. A cave and the rooms had
that sensation of pink.

He gets up for the bathroom –

asked Brendan Kennelly the other day
if he liked his father. I don't score.
Memories, vows, of other people ...

Heavy knocking on the door.
The old sister. Time to depart.
He's sick. He puts his hand
in his pocket – "Here's a
few shillings to get a taxi".

Kisses hidden in the wallpaper.

She leads him away in his braces.

Who was on the hall linoleum
making farewell?

Vergil in a robe, Dante in
a nightshirt? Gregory VII with
Kerry tiara eyes? Pearse unshot
mellow? Sam young, drunk,
structurally heterosexual
the perfect compliment?

MacGreevy!

YEATS:
NEW WAYS OF FALLING IN LOVE

"If we cannot imagine ourselves as different
from what we are, and try to assume the
second self, we cannot impose a discipline
upon ourselves though we may accept one
from others. Active virtue, as distinguished
from the passive acceptance of a code, is
therefore theatrical, consciously dramatic, the
wearing of a mask ..."

Hic. Let us talk of Yeats at last since we grew
up with him, and he was our first dandy.
Since what poetry we have comes from his
seeds, the seeds of sacred trees, mediterranean
olives, post-solar systems, the seeds of men. A
week does not go by, after sixty years, that his
name does not appear in newspaper or
journal. I show them to my students.

Ille. His shade is in our spirit life. I study his
spells and wishes with great diligence, I look
askance at Irish contemporaries, I slap the
current laureate's wrist for his reservations,
"waywardness and eccentric beliefs". What is

missing from Seamus: he learned from everyone except Yeats, the teacher of religious studies. No Sutras or Gospels up his sleeves, Seamus can be a dull writer. Waywardness in muse-pursuit cannot be eccentric, look at the punk spray on Pegasus's wing. Those astral marshals, Yeats and Wilde, blitzed us for ever, punks not the Dublin tinsel crowd in the paddock.

Hic. I am indebted to that watery knight Stephen Spender for a definition of influence, "The felt presence of his (Yeats's) as a spirit working in the writing of other poets". Spender says such a figure does two things, 1) states the accurate external situation which can be adapted by the listening poet and 2) carries over the words used, the rhythms, and finally the attitude. Attitudes, let us wear them. Our mask life in Ireland prepared us for all events, Stateside the disguises are not theatrical, they do not cut into the face, comic joy does not pour in the night glasses.

Ille. Eberhardt and Roethke skate in a colonnade technically flotsam. Did Roethke ever wear Diversion? He tried sailing the sea and landed at Byzantium Pub & Restaurant, Island of the Blessed, Co. Galway. Tried to shine real hymns in twilight wind and pier shrine to havoc, indulgence, hangover, and redemption by ballad metre where the

contrived voice can discover soul. Roethke's
use of Yeats's neo-Rabelaisian ballad
pyrotechnics means not only late flowering
drunk love at first sight but conversion to the
idea of poetry community. Almost some other
self, partner of joy.

Hic. John Montague's story has him almost
getting there. Ted was introduced to George
Yeats and then demanded that Beatrice his
wife be a medium. The occult as marriage
counsellor! Bless me, great crystal, I have
consulted you, but do not know what glass
face to wear. Our friend Eamonn Wall, now in
splendor in St. Louis, bless his incognitos,
speaks of how magical Irish landscapes can
present themselves in American suburbs. He
evidences the example of the
Stevens-MacGreevy postcard, sea-worn Cliffs
of Moher to fine insurance paper. Eavan
Boland defines this fatal attraction,
"Something or someone – Yeats, an ethos, call
it what you will – seems to have written the
script for those hills and valleys, those
reflections on Atlantic rain and misty
prospects".

Ille. You and I, in differing ways, promenade
the Mid-Atlantic card as if we had picked it
up from the bushes at St. Brendan's well,
never came back from the fair with the cattle
like our grandfather did and made for the

boat. A sup of the Saints' Well, Beckett couldn't resist it. Yeats often rocked back and forth in currents; Anglo-Irish water polo masks. I bring Niedecker into this, for she had a lamp in which she could see the river ebb and flow. I believe Lorine, river run lady, beheld Yeats as maker of lake and bird pastorals and inhabitant of the ultimate romantic house boat. Lonely and Zukofsky-spurned, banished by abortion from New York, her triste "Paean to Place" arises from swim practice on Black Hawk Island, Fort Atkinson. Innisfree was still and churned, as much as Thoreau's pond. Her "floating life" on chaos builds her writing strength, from Haiku to serial poem, on early reading, "Books/ at home-pier/Shelley could steer as he read ...". As the liberation point performs, a Yeats quotation modified delivers the reader to the pathos of her parents' marriage, "Roped not 'looped/in the loop/of her hair'". On a river bank opening into the big lake: rain, snow, flood around her shack, as though a motte and bailey, she was not a Princess in a tower but presence among the boats and landings. In winter the onlooker of bowling played on the frozen river. Robinson Jeffers went to Thor Ballylee, "Yeats wasn't there, nobody was, all the shutters up, he was present". Niedecker took from The Tower, the historical external situation. Pound also thundered by Cathay rivers. She apotheosised Jefferson, Darwin, Morris; her Morris explains, "Yeats saw the betterment of the

workers/by religion-slow in any case as the
drying of the moon/he was not understood
..."

Hic. I want to leave Lorine, you share with
W.B. a liking for powerful women, even in
shoals like that. I've seen you cozying up to
the women bar owners of Milwaukee,
barstooling to other side beauty. I want to
return to the male hunt for Yeats; its
controversies; Berryman is the master of
hounds. I saw this yelping cloud as it hit
Dublin: son to father, world-tourist to world
traveller. Two inquiries moved Berryman
1), the test of any romantic poet, "strange
poems made under the shadow of death", the
elder passed with his "honey breath".
2) was Berryman fully at home with, could he
stay in, the moon-run *A Vision*'s heaven and
hell? Berryman found the Christian self, he
whips past the Anglo-Irish shaman to "feu!
feu! feu!" "It is plain to me/*Christ* underwent
man & treachery & socks & lashes, thirst,
exhaustion, the bit, for *my* pathetic &
disgusting vices". Of course Yeats could select
the extraordinary voice out of Aramaic air.
Berryman's Dublin agenda may be not just to
connect to the personage he drank tea with
long ago but to be a pilgrim to that ruined
Pagan and Catholic country looming behind
the tea cups.

Ille. The American poets landed in Ireland to kiss those feet, whether they belonged to a living man or not. Ireland, the mask behind Yeats's personality, they worshipped. Even Niedecker did and she was a backyard ritualist. Berryman laid his homages in person (Dantesque gifts), Jeffers earlier had offered equal rhetoric. Jeffers was the most authentic Yeatsian, Protestant and reactionary like his master, skeptical in the midst of a huge urge to transcendence. "The heavy black stones of the cairn of the Lord of Ulster./A man of blood who died bloodily/Four centuries ago: but death's nothing, and life,/From a high death-mark on a headland/Of this dim island of burials, is nothing either./How beautiful are both these nothings". Blessed is nothing because of nothing but Yeats had Plato and Plotinus, the cavalcade of muse-dished philosophers, mad philosophy hurt him into song. Yeats's cleverness lay in refusing to be intimidated into being an intellectual, he kept memory for his poetry, and his prose as an introduction to his poems. There was no market place, only his place. He created Zion anywhere as he wished. Aristocratic women bore him songs. Lord of the swings and roundabouts. He bowed to Modernism, it bowed back. On the headlands he wore longer seer's eyes out to sea, the ancient priest of Drumcliff. The antic hay of poet's fields.

Hic. Charm has saved him for ever.

Ille. Yeats also played the fool and that perhaps is what the United States is not good at!

Hic. Back to the beginning. We started in Dublin, in the back seat with our parents to Sligo, rowed on Lough Gill while Daddy got out his movie camera, we glimpsed London before we had a drink, we saw the Tower before its terrible renovation when cows were inside but its walls were cobalt blue. The poet was still there, not the Tourist Board. All was theatre and all was pure.

Ille. Brought up on Yeats – how else would I know anything about poetry or Ireland? Brought up on Michael Collins – how else would I know anything about history or Ireland? The two Irelands we still deal with, Declan Kiberd's implausibilities are not mine. Yeats on my mother's bedside table beside the crucifix, Michael Collins on the mantlepiece beside the bottle of scotch ... We used to go looking for mushrooms in the fields in September when rain began the release of Celtic winter. Druid mushrooms but actually the domestic kind. A ritual not much focused on, like Yeats's wand-picking hands that basically opened a new scene to poetry in English. What I saw was Yeats as the gatekeeper to the field of mushrooms.

Hic. Perhaps he was also the disheveled angel who crept into mother's sleep after the good Christian angel had left.

Ille. We lived on the wings of the 1890's; we overheard the dinner talk of those Christmas pals, Wilde and Yeats. One golden trumpet fell silent by cruelty, the other one (the lucky one) opened up more, and then he and his café pal, Ezra I nearly said Extra Pound, became the guardians of modernism that was so bright and posh in the new written imagination.

Hic. Spells hand on spells! From the early impressionistic folk wakes of a country turning its ways, as now, into modes for a new century to a later top shelf effect. Fancy dress impressed the United States from the start but some of our poets were hushed then angry. The litany: oak tree too big, romance of our personal/sexual sun moon stars too pointed, not enough victimisation to go around.

Ille. The local poets are getting around to look again. Eavan Boland is fair to him, she glimpses underneath the constructed poetic selfhood the man stumbles into old age, humiliation, illumination. Recognition nothing can stop his singing mouth. Soul

clapping its hands abolishes the wake. The
only completely lovely poet since Yeats,
Kavanagh (the other K completes the trinity of
greatness) says it best, "One living poem
written each year can redeem a whole school
of writers from death. During the lifetime of
Yeats that living poem appeared again and
again, and as it flashed the dead bodies stirred
with desire". Gratitude to the dancing flame
of Medbh McGuckian who when pressed on
the usual charge that Yeats's world "was a
quasi-feudal one inhabited by ideal peasants,
ideal aristocrats and ideal artists", replied,
"I'd almost subscribe to it once the emphasis
was on the word ideal".

Hic. The dead bodies stirred with desire.

"Because I seek an image, not a book.
Those men that in their writing are most wise
Own nothing but their blind, stupefied hearts,
I call to the mysterious one who yet
Shall walk the wet sands by the edge of the
    stream …"

DAWN

"Waugh was with me at Oxford
he wore a yellow sweater everywhere
he was a nancy boy ..."

I look up to a bulldog face
Christopher Hollis a Tory member
of Parliament

a Catholic – I've been a Catholic
for forty years
slouching in a yellow sweater

morning and noon –
yellow sweater not star for Jonathon
yellow sweater not star for David

Davy Byrnes's pub a fragment
forty years ago.

SWOONING

In the soil of their almost
forsakable bodies

running into the fields
seed or no seed that is not the point

the light beyond privacy sends up a flare
can the sun dance and fold its legs

can the sun die and dance
a place the sun beats a very early wave length.

To heat praises beside the fire
to sit on the couch with the odes:

Christopher Isherwood, you had the best
    non-movie sex in Hollywood.
Robert Duncan, you were the laundry beside
    the closet.
And San Francisco, you were the
    lighthouse/bathhouse.
Nora Barnacle, you were as right as the
    Galway rain.

And, Clare Reeves, you loved someone
   besides father.
Bill Burroughs, you were Kiki's sweet sugar
   daddy.
James Joyce, we watched you perform on the
   canal bank.
Scariff, you saw Merriman coming.

FRANCIS

Most beautiful Englishman ever to live in
    Ireland
the importance of being earnest angry and
    funny a big brother/sister

roar in the mike body
pour blood inside it
glue and blood alright
no burning backroom tiger
or take it from behind
that burning

Shoot the museum
that serves doughnuts and coffee
"Get something here for 15 cents
in Pittsburgh we have a few Bacons
we keep them locked up
they're like August
the dead heat of August
dead meat so beautiful you eat it"

Who made the mistake
to let the Jesuits
use "Jesus"
(The Pope is the supreme art critic
Jesus a romancer)

Boys some kind of lilies
a paint harem
where do we put the clothes
we take off

George Dyer was crucified in your arms
fruit burnt motive burnt
we move in the fire with Arjuna's charioteer
"He who seeks worklessness in work
and works in worklessness enjoys
only god dreams
at any moment one is not free
except for one's shame
only one's shame"

Darling you understand that inside each Pope
      there is a monk
who unwraps chocolate the more beautiful
      the meat the more libidinous the knife
besides these wenches were in another
      country and were men

Look what I have done with the country
      inside me

TRIPTYCH 2002

Protestant nymph
later the chandelier painted purple

Old screamers/old songsters
"No god but one can become man"

Yellow throne
Pius
sedia gestoria shadow perch

two owls of Minerva on the back of the throne
vibrant casting

from antiquity
rule of the oracles

"Do prophecies still come from Delphi"

Two owls of Minerva on the back of the
    throne

Am I not
a Pope like you
are you not
Jesus like me

Communion with the dead meat on the cross
brutality is there incoherence
thick voodoo bristles

fencing lessons
which is how to drink more
they kill us for our port

Meat home
R.I.C. carcasses
hanging on a gate
outside Lord Mayo's great house

Chalice or bowl of blood hanging by the wood
betrayal abandonment atonement
champagne moves all meat

"Darling all the faces I've painted
I've met in pubs"

Keen body wake-paint

wet

a four star alert
of male bodies

a boy made of a star inside Venus
perfumes out of the sea

"When you're young the sea
can fill you with hope"

Degas put the sea by the riders

Jesus Christ is Nada Nada lives for ever Nada
    is Jesus Christ

Rose thou art shadow
Ark of the slaughterhouse
House of gold

at the foot of the cross the oracle screams

You seek images for the thing you desire
love kills you

Priest in white and yellow over there
Youth in the great Irish stables

THE LORD'S PASSION,
MARCH 24, 2002

It is strange to think of what he says on the
cross. (In Hebrew, or in some form of
Aramaic) he cries out what is not possible,
Lord, why have you deserted me? How could
this be? Jesus went willingly to death in
conformity with the father's will, to heal sin
and share death. He must have known what
he had to do and yet at the moment of
sacrifice he accuses the father of
abandonment.

At this Confirmation time the Catholic kids of
Southeastern Wisconsin write letters to me, I
get a kick out of reading them; but it is not
easy. Recently I came across lines like this,
where was God when my grandmother died,
when my parents got divorced where was
God, when Dad lost his job why did God
allow that?

I tell them it seems we are left but we must
keep faith.

This Lent we ask the same question. Why
have we been abandoned? The Catholic
Church is nailed on the cross, it is chastised
and scourged, reviled before the people –
Archbishop Rembert Weakland presiding

LINES PENNED AT THE MEMORIAL LIBRARY, MADISON, ON THE OCCASION OF THE CENTENARY OF OSCAR WILDE

In the post-Wagnerian world we make
    restitution to the divinities

Man's first and last disobedience apparent in
    the divinities

Great ballroom ringed with laughter floor of
    the Hall of Infamy

Wallflower ghosts of queers seated by the
    Avoca river

Rise

Billy who took the tickets in the Paramount
    Cinema
harassed to suicide
dance

Young Quirke with a bad leg beaten on the
    street
afraid to go out at night
dance

All of you learn to dance now

Start moving them singing lips

be smart send everything out as an aria

move around reciting on the grassy bank

last obscure performance be first Ritzy one

(rocking not walking on the water)

turn toasts into prayers for dead souls

shabby and unknown in your hunger cross
    over a line

ON THE STATUS OF EVIL FLOWERS

Outside the Church there are not enough
    taboos or wrong tendernesses.
150 years later no shift is needed from Evil
    Flowers' energy deviance:
19th century gay and lesbian thrills were
    greater than 20th century ones.

(Don't forget your flowers at St. Valentine's,
    Zack)

Book as receptacle, innocence kicked in the
    teeth.
Literature as arson. Readers who guess what
    rotten teeth
Vergil's shepherds laid on each other.

Three kinds of writers: those strong enough to
    find
old glitter to throw, those sly to get some
    flames shooting by,
chanters of all night litanies that don't dim
    their car lights.

Gold Set Dancing, small sparks?

Pages that should be atrocious
against dead and living creatures
on their golfing routes.
Kid, sweat out your liver.

My Mother was a New Yorker, My Bishop Rembert Weakland & a Valentine

I see in the late afternoon light
St. Valentine,
I see in the clear Cathedral hour
Archbishop Weakland's word light:

"I still ask how can I love
a God, who could
be a figure of my imagination?
I realise I love my mother
love her still
though she is not tangible.
In fact I confess that after her death
I continue to talk with her
at least once a week as I used to,
but it is cheaper since I do not have
to pay for a long distance phone call.
Yet my conversations with God
seem to be a bit one-sided, I hope
He/She is a good listener".

My monologue, lover, in
the gleaning moment
on the Park Place bedspread:

"Mother's hands and words
taking this night now
speaking silver-breasted
blessed be a Rose of Riverside Drive
blessed be body that gives me body
blessed be hands that gave me hands".
St. Valentine, enjoin.

MEMORIES OF THE LONDON ZOO

I feel like Pontius Pilate
I wash my hands and they come
out in elegies
I can't wash the elegies off
my body.
Are people indelible?

I ran across the road outside the Zoo
with my sister and my father slapped us.

We were nearly killed in Regents Park
but we got out of Kensington in time.

I saw from our window the dome of St. Paul's
thought Cranmer and Donne had flown it in
    by cargo plane.

Charles Dickens frightened me, I read
his hot Protestant Child's History of England.

Saw from the window the Queen driving in
the gate of Holland House barrage balloons
    overhead.

Antique-loving German Queen Mary
not a stone to be left of the temple of the
    Whigs.

Cranmer and Donne opened their mouths
and caught the German planes in them.

I put my memories of Lazarus into the river
the rivulets that run into the Irish Sea.

"Is it possible there is no other memory
but the memory of wounds" – which
    wounds?

Is it possible there is no other memory
than the memory of waiting near a Zoo?

No memory but the memory of being an
    animal
nothing but that of being in a cage?

FOR THE GENTLEMAN

A white carnation is an ever present
metaphor; the door of metaphor
is kicked in, a glass on the
plain table, yours.

Raise the glass,
you're leaved and veined.

In that act of darkness or novelty
when the lights go out,
what you're left with is a high voice.
An obituary is burnt into flowers …
There are two more items for the gentleman,

water hopping with words, forest that
　　shutters
flowers: to begin with, we were ·
college students working on Beowulf,
next step was an Anglo-Saxon hymn,
first words imitated first words.

Make them shine like Baptism,
the water is melancholy;

there's a bell ringing in it; bells ringing
in the flowers too. I want to speak
in code to all who know something.
You hold a flower in your lapel like
the Buddha, you picked it in the wood.

Don't sigh, give me your glass,
the universe is poured out in six days.
On the seventh Wilde appears
drummer and genie, double rap of the
    sequence
in the swampy forest, you hear him

at those hymns. Nevertheless a sure thing,
he knows singing, 30-inch wingspan.

PHOTO

The only photograph I ever took
was the plaque being laid and flowered
on Wilde's house Westland Row 1954

Eggs flew from behind a bus
missed Lennox Robinson
and MacLiammoir at the door

About liberation you asked yourself
    that day –
what about being an erotic person
you have no management

except your skin and the curve of a libido
you've got to use your mouth
first

be in a towering passion
for a poet bows out of a chocolate book
which is why they must disappear inside a
    lens

so they remain cold and hardy
I stood in fog and justice on Westland Row
I saw two Bay islands

one clad in fog the other lit with justice
seagulls mermaids sailors
the music hall ditty

"The world is straighter and more Protestant
than you imagine"
I stood up then and took the photo

The Wilde house on Westland Row, Dublin.
Lennox Robinson is plainly in view,
MacLiammoir is a bit hidden.

(Photo taken by James Liddy, 1954)

Afterword

"Alien Primitive and Dionysian": Some Thoughts on James Liddy

Michael S. Begnal

"I'm trying to write in such a way that nobody else would write", James Liddy told me when I interviewed him at Coolgreany, Co. Wexford a year ago. "That's the example of Baudelaire, and I think one must always be different". But this can be a risky proposition for an Irish poet – Ireland is a country where the weight of its poetic tradition is heavier than most. Only recently has the conservatism of the last century begun to yield in any significant way. If a poet like Thomas MacGreevy can still linger in semi-oblivion, what then of Liddy? ("It takes an Irish person to know how difficult/it is to be Irish", he writes in his new collection). For the American poet John Ashbery, though, his singularity is the mark of his greatness:

> I consider him to be one of the most original among living Irish poets, perhaps the most. His work has not received the attention accorded his more famous contemporaries ... but I am convinced of its superiority.

We can only hope that Brian Arkins' recent critical study of Liddy (published by Arlen House in 2001) has gone some way towards redressing the imbalance.

Here in this book, Liddy himself confesses that he looks "askance" at his contemporaries, and "slap[s] the current laureate's wrist". That would be Heaney's. "Seamus can be a dull writer", he says, and it's about time that someone did. To be boring is the greatest sin that a poet can commit, and this much I know – James Liddy is never boring. It's not my aim, however, to boost my subject by reproving a Nobel Prize winner or anyone else. That is Liddy's prerogative in the poem in question ("Yeats: New Ways of Falling in Love"), but I find the special pleading that some of his supporters tend to revert to wholly unnecessary (though certainly understandable – on the one hand an expression of affection for the poet, and on the other, shock in the face of popular ignorance).

I say if it is his fate to remain an outsider, then so be it. Thus he remains dangerous and potent. An on-the-run priest at the Mass Rock. He has his readers; he will have more. He does not crave critical acceptance, only the regard of his friends. Listen: "I am alien primitive and/Dionysian and my poems/curate portrait galleries where nude lovers/flourish". Poetry at its root is ecstatic, as primitive religion is ecstatic. Indeed they spring from the *same* root. For Liddy, the figure of Yeats is the "gatekeeper to the field of mushrooms". Who can understand this? Other poets, perhaps ...

This poet (Liddy) will not be conveniently categorized, and he sometimes confounds even his own fans. One of Ireland's foremost gay poets, he is also an unabashed Catholic. He knows that "you don't like this, nobody rational/can", but Liddy isn't particularly interested in the rational. Does he contradict himself? Very well then he contradicts himself. Like Whitman he is large, he contains multitudes. Rather than rationality or consistency, he is instead interested in beauty, in adoration, in love, in ritual: "The aroma of the bazaar is/missing from 'enlightenment'". His Catholicism is not dogmatic or moralistic; it's antinomian (look it up if you don't know). "The Pope is the supreme art critic" – no one but Liddy could get away with that!

Though I suspect his intention isn't to be a poster boy for a movement, Liddy is, as Arkins put it, "no closet homosexual". His outsider poetic stance must in no small way be connected with his vision of himself as a sexual outlaw. He identifies with Oscar Wilde. On Wilde's centenary he remembers "Billy ... harassed to suicide" and "Quirke with a bad leg beaten on the/street/afraid to go out at night". He remembers the admonition given to him in 1954 during the dedication of the plaque at the Wilde house, Dublin: "The world is straighter and more Protestant than you imagine". Let us not forget that this whole volume is subtitled "Wilde Centenary Poems".

The main title of the new collection, *I Only Know That I Love Strength in My Friends and Greatness*, I believe perfectly sums up James' outlook on life at this moment in time. This statement, borrowed from Jack Spicer, is in his mouth simultaneously compassionate (Catholic) and heroic (pagan). He lauds friends and fellow poets (often one and the same), so here we have tributes to the "territories" of Spicer, Hartnett, Rimbaud, Jarry, Bowen, Burroughs, Kerouac and others. Jack Kerouac (another antinomian, incidentally) is essential to any appreciation of Liddy's milieu. That's a strange thing to say about an Irish writer, for the Irish have never properly understood Kerouac (perhaps another reason why they haven't really understood Liddy either). With Yeats and Kavanagh, he completes a "trinity of greatness".

Like Kerouac, Liddy's subject is ultimately himself, and his poetic form is dictated solely by the organic flow of his consciousness. After you read, close your eyes, see. "I pan your mind cells,/your internal system, grains of ordinary/existence turn into gold ...". This singular consciousness, the mind of the poet, this "I" of the poems, is a lens through which we can view the cosmos, or history perhaps – Irish history, poetic history, an erotic history.

It is overtly autobiographical but it doesn't depend on the reader being able to "relate" to the poet in every detail. One need not be gay, Catholic, or Irish (or even American) to love James Liddy, just as one need not be black to love John Coltrane or a woman to love Frida Kahlo.

It is now nearly forty years since The Dolmen Press brought out James Liddy's first collection, *In a Blue Smoke* (1964). In that time he's published numerous other books, but for me this latest one ranks up there among his best. Poets often peak early, establishing a degree of renown by producing a few poems that resonate in some way, but to which "the later work" then tends to be unfavourably compared. It is gratifying to know that James has not yet reached his zenith but, like a glass being raised in perpetual salutation, continues to ascend, ascend, ascend.

Note

The title of this collection comes from a poem of
Jack Spicer's
"A Poem Without A Single Bird in it"
sent to Robin Blaser in Boston
13 December 1956